THE
FISCAL
THERAPY

SOLUTION 1.0

THE
FISCAL
THERAPY

SOLUTION 1.0

SIX STEPS TO PERSONAL AND BUSINESS FINANCIAL HEALTH

MARC J. BERNSTEIN
JD, CHFC®, CLU®, CAP®

Printed in the United States of America

Library of Congress Control Number: 2018947595

Paperback ISBN: 978-1-947368-77-4
eBook ISBN: 978-1-947368-78-1

Cover Design: Zeljka Kojic
Interior Design: Ghislain Viau

"Marc has been a lifetime learner throughout his professional career of over 30 years. This book gives us an opportunity to learn from some of Marc's experiences and implement these strategies for our own financial goals, our businesses and our families. Marc's views on fiscal therapy are just what is needed to help us take control of our financial goals and aspirations."

— DAVID LABRICCIOSA,
MANAGING DIRECTOR ASPIREWEALTH PLANNERS*

"Financial freedom is a goal sought out by many but without a disciplined plan, it is difficult to achieve. With the fiscal therapy approach you can work to develop a plan that works for you."

—DAVID O'MALLEY
PRESIDENT & COO OF PENN MUTUAL LIFE INSURANCE COMPANY*

"This is a book that needed to be written. It is equally relevant to be read by prospective clients wanting to know more about what process a true financial professional uses. The process focuses on what clients want. Their goals dreams and aspirations. Products, performance, and sophisticated transactions are subordinate to the goals of the clients. It is also a great manual for financial practitioners to show them how to become a trusted advisor. Well done Marc Bernstein!"

—JOSEPH W JORDAN
WORLD RENOWNED AUTHOR & LECTURER

"I've been in the financial services industry for over 25 years, and this is the process that gives people what they want to move them towards financial independence."

—JAMES J. MEEHAN
MSM MANAGING PARTNER, 1847FINANCIAL,
AND CURRENT CHAIRMAN OF THE BOARD OF AMERICAN COLLEGE*

"Marc's 'Fiscal Therapy' process has it right. It first asks, 'Who are you and what do you want to do?' Then, the money. Usually it's the other way around."

—RAY LOEWE, THE LUCKIEST GUY IN THE WORLD

"The legendary coach John Wooden defined true success as, "The peace of mind that comes from the self-assurance of knowing you are doing the best you can do to become the best you are capable of becoming." The Fiscal Therapy Solution by Marc Bernstein, clearly lays out a tried and true path for financial wellbeing that when followed will bring you the freedom that comes from knowing you are experiencing true success."

—LEE BROWER, FOUNDER AND CHIEF INNOVATION OFFICER,
EMPOWERED WEALTH, LC

*David O'Malley is President and COO of Penn Mutual Life Insurance Company. David LaBricciosa is the Managing Director of AspireWealth Planners, a Penn Mutual affiliated office. James J. Meehan is MSM Managing Partner of Penn's Philadelphia agency, 1847Financial. Penn Mutual and its affiliate offices are not endorsing The Fiscal Therapy Solution. The above quotes are the ideas of the individuals that provided them. (They are not intended to show or provide any bias toward Marc Bernstein and The Fiscal Therapy Solution.)

ACKNOWLEDGEMENTS

I am fortunate to have been raised by parents who provided me with a solid support system and who spoke to my brothers and I often about money, business and finance and who provided us with all that we needed, as well as great educations. Thanks to my Mom, Joan for her constant love and support. And to my Dad, Irv, of blessed memory, for his fatherly love and consistent lessons, including one of the basic principles underlying this book, "Pay yourself first."

I am also fortunate to have married my best friend and partner in life, Susan, who is always there for me, and has provided unconditional love through it all. My gratitude goes out to her for riding the roller coaster of life with me (and she doesn't like roller coasters!). Also, thanks to our children, Jake and Dara. They were patient with my long hours and devotion to the building of my business and to my related interests. As a family, we love to travel together, and they are great companions on this journey of life.

It would have been much more difficult to complete this project without the assistance and focus of my business manager, Heather Page. I am not always easy (a somewhat obvious admission to those who know me well) and her patience, devotion and loyalty have been invaluable.

To my partners and associates at MWealth Advisors, you are all participating in the great Fiscal Therapy laboratory/experience and your partnership, friendship, and principled approach to financial planning has reaffirmed my commitment to the process. I am fortunate to be in an industry that shares, teaches and provides great opportunities for lifelong learning through such organizations as the Million Dollar Round Table, Forum 400, AALU, the Financial Planning Association etc. I want to give thanks to the leadership teams and associates of AspireWealth Planners and of 1847Financial. Their leaders, David (Dave)LaBricciosa and James (Jim) Meehan, are my long term business associates and friends, and I am grateful for the continuing opportunity to teach and learn with them and their organizations. This is also a wonderful opportunity to thank all of the mentors and friends I've had the opportunity to be associated with over a long sustained career.

Acknowledgements

Thanks to the Strategic Coach organization for providing a structured approach to learning and dynamic growth and for the many ideas accumulated from the materials, coaches and fellow journey men and women that have, among other things, inspired my writing of this book. Thanks, in particular, to fellow "coachee", Ray Loewe, author of "The Luckiest Guy in the World", for his encouragement to follow through with my idea and complete this book.

Lastly, thanks to you, for taking the time to read and perhaps, think about a different approach to thinking about and planning your financial future and legacy.

CONTENTS

AN INVITATION

Imagine for a moment that money is abundant. Your wallet might be full, your account balances could be healthy, and you're feeling good. Imagine that you no longer spend your time worrying about money; instead, you spend your time enjoying it. I'm happy to say that this small book is an invitation to look at money in a new way. For most people, money is the subject of constant worry—whether or not they have anything to worry about. In my experience, even very wealthy people tend to spend a disproportionate amount of time thinking and worrying about money. That's because many of us were raised to have an uneasy relationship with financial matters. Consider just the simple term "cold, hard cash" or the much more dramatic saying that "money is the root of all evil." Why do we talk about money in such unfavorable terms? Why don't we regard it, instead, with a feeling of warmth and abundance?

The answer is that we've never been given a chance to think of it that way because many of us were taught from a young age that money is bad or sinful or taught to be afraid because it will someday run out. That means that as adults we end up spending a lot of our time feeling anxious about money—even as we spend little or no time trying to reprogram our minds to look at money in a different way.

Until now. This book is about a process of "fiscal therapy" in which you may partner with a trusted advisor to build a solid plan for helping turn your dreams and financial goals into reality. You'll also recondition the way your heart and mind regard money, cultivating a new approach: a sense that you're meant to have money and intend to have it in abundance.

You are surely familiar with the saying that success is a journey rather than a destination. That truism plays a role in fiscal therapy. In this process, we generally don't think of some point out on the horizon as the single driving goal. Instead, fiscal therapy is an ongoing journey in which we build security and financial freedom and in which you are, we hope, enjoying your money all along the way. Oftentimes people think in terms of a set number, believing that once they reach that specific income or net worth they will finally have arrived. But that sort of mindset can get you into trouble. You can easily fall into a trap of thinking that spending money is just plain bad (it isn't), and you can end up focusing so much on a future number that you forget to experience the present. Life is too short for that.

The truth is that there's no end point to success. In the fiscal therapy approach, you can build a plan with us to assist you in helping you achieve financial freedom. We'll also try to help you enjoy the process, and your money, along the way.

Let's get started.

KG9460

Chapter One

WHAT BROUGHT YOU HERE?

You're reading this book for a reason. Maybe you don't feel as though your finances are truly in order. Maybe it bothers you that you haven't updated your will and estate plans. Or maybe you lie awake at night wondering whether you're saving enough to meet your financial needs in retirement. Or if you have plenty of money, do you worry what to do with it or have guilt about what you're *not* doing with it?

Don't worry, because you're not alone. In my experience, I've observed that most people spend more time worrying about money than they ever do planning their finances. They're constantly thinking about providing for their family by earning money at a job or running a business, paying for unexpected expenses, managing their credit, and saving enough for their kids' college education and for their own retirement, too. But the time spent worrying about all these things is often way out of proportion to the time spent creating or tending to a solid plan. Whereas if people instead set aside just a little bit of time to actually do that organized planning, perhaps they could finally stop worrying.

Happily, you have now begun that process. You may be reading this book because you're looking for assistance in creating and coordinating a comprehensive financial plan. You may be reading because you have concerns regarding your business or personal financial situation. Or you're reading because you want someone else—someone with experience and a reality-based approach—to help care for you and your money. Well, no matter what reason brought you to this book today, my hope is that you're now on your way to less worrying and much greater security and independence.

I learned from a young age how deeply important that security is. When I was growing up, my dad worked for himself, having built a company in the wholesale greeting card business. For decades, he had worked hard to build his business and to provide for our family, and when I was in high school, he was just beginning to think about slowing down and moving toward retirement. At the same time, he had been meaning to update the insurance policy he carried for his business. But he was a busy man and a dedicated father, and he just hadn't quite gotten around to updating that policy.

Then we got the phone call that would change our lives for years to come.

His business was in a warehouse building that housed several other companies. One day, when I was a senior in high school, we got the call that the warehouse had gone up in flames. A fire that had started two doors down—at a paint company—had spread throughout the building. We rushed to the scene.

I'll never forget standing outside my dad's business and watching the firefighters try to save the building. My dad was relatively calm during this disaster, even though he had come from extremely modest beginnings and had built the business with his own hands. He had often worked seven days a week when

I was growing up. Now he watched the whole thing go up in flames. It's the stuff of nightmares. And as we stood there and watched, he told me that updating his business insurance had been on his list of things to do—but that he had not done it.

Now he was afraid the existing insurance wouldn't be enough to cover the damages from the fire.

And he was right. That fire ruined everything. Whatever the flames hadn't eaten was ruined by water or smoke, and the insurance didn't nearly cover it.

My dad was in his fifties at that time, and he had just started to think about spending more time enjoying life. Now he would have to start all over again.

In the weeks and months after the fire, he began trying to figure out how to pick up the pieces. What was he going to do? I remember going out for a walk with him during that time. He had been thinking about what it would take to rebuild his business, and I remember what he said to me.

"I don't think I can do it," he said, shaking his head. "I think I want to hang it up." He told me that he'd been offered a job at a greeting card company in Kansas City and that our family might be moving there. (My reaction to this announcement was a purely selfish one: "I'm not moving," I told him. I was in a band and had a girlfriend, and I didn't plan on relocating to Missouri. I'm not proud of that reaction, but I suppose I was just acting like the teenager I was.) I had enough maturity, I guess, that we continued to discuss the pros and cons of packing up and moving.

In the end, my dad didn't take that job in Kansas City. He thought about it long and hard, and finally he decided that he would go back to the business he'd built and that he would build it up all over again. He would have to move to a new warehouse, which was going to be more expensive, so all his costs were going to go up. He also needed to replace everything he'd lost: his whole inventory. And to make this new plan work, meet his own financial goals, and continue to be the strong provider he had always been for our family, he determined that he would now have to *triple* the size of his business—just to get back to where he had been. That's what I remember most vividly. In his mid-fifties, he was going to start all over again, and he was going to have to work *harder* this time.

You know what? He did it. It set him back quite a few years, but eventually he did what he had set out to do. He tripled the size of his business.

In the pages ahead, you're going to learn about what I call the "fiscal therapy" approach to financial planning, in which you'll define what financial freedom means to you, and in which we'll build protection into your plan as one of our first priorities. We'll focus on creating financial success in your life— helping reduce the chance that an unforeseen emergency doesn't force you to rebuild late in life. We call this process of discovery and planning "fiscal therapy" because there are many similarities between financial planning and health care, which we'll get into in the pages ahead, and because it has a ring to it. The word "fiscal" normally refers to government finances, but it can apply to personal finances as well. The term "fiscal therapy" is easy to remember, and I believe it hits home based on my conversations with clients and others in more casual conversations.

I learned a great deal from my dad's experience, including that even the most skillful and dedicated business owners and breadwinners need good protection. It's no accident that I'm a financial planner. I didn't take a direct path to get here; I certainly didn't know, back when I was a teenager telling my dad that I wasn't going to Kansas City, that I would become a planner. In fact, after taking Accounting 101, and working in the accounting office at The University of Delaware as a college intern, I vowed not to become an accountant, which was what my grandfather and uncle had done. In college I majored in music, and after college, I went to law school. But I soon realized that being an attorney wasn't my true calling. More than thirty years ago, when I became a financial advisor, I found my mission. Ever since, I have set out to help people build the financial security that every family, and every business, should have.

The First Step on the Path to Financial Health

As you begin your journey to financial wellness, the first step is to consider what financial health means to you. It means something different for everyone, and the circumstances of your financial life, and what you ultimately hope to achieve, will be unique to you.

When a prospective client first gives me a call to explore the possibility of beginning fiscal therapy, the first thing I always ask is, "What made you decide to come see me?" I want to know where you're coming from and what motivated you to pick up the phone. As part of this initial introduction, I ask a series of questions, including, "What are you trying to accomplish? What would have to happen in our first meeting such that you'd walk out of it and say 'Hey, we had a really good outcome from this encounter'?"

Your journey begins here.

STEP 1
DEFINE YOUR PURPOSE: WHAT DOES FINANCIAL HEALTH MEAN TO YOU?

You may not know precisely what your definition of financial health is at this moment. That's okay; there's still a lot you *do* know. Set aside some time and think about what success in this process would mean to you. What does "financial freedom" mean on your own terms? Be as specific as you can. When you have a sense of your answer, jot it down. It may change over time, of course, and that's to be expected. What matters right now is that you've taken the first step toward financial wellness by defining your purpose.

In the pages ahead, we're going to cover the steps to financial health in detail, and you'll learn about the "fiscal therapy" approach—in which dreams plus financial data become the raw material for building solid plans backed by numbers. But, hopefully, you've already begun a new era of your own, one in which you might turn any fear and unease about money into a new sense of security and abundance.

THIS CHAPTER IN BRIEF

▲ The "fiscal therapy" approach to financial planning converts dreams and financial data into solid plans backed by numbers.

▲ In this process, we'll focus on creating financial success in your life. That includes an emphasis on protection, in which we'll help to ensure that an unforeseen emergency doesn't force you to rebuild late in life.

▲ The first step in fiscal therapy is to consider what financial freedom means to you. Set aside some time to think about this, and then jot down your thoughts. (It's okay if your answer changes over time!) Be as specific as you can.

Chapter Two

GETTING TO KNOW YOU

Once you've defined your initial purpose, the second step on the road to financial wellness is an assessment of your current situation—but not (yet) all the details of your financial data. Because genuine financial wellness has at least as much to do with your personality and life circumstances as it does with numbers and financial instruments, I believe it is essential that the financial advisor first spend time getting a detailed view of the client's life and trajectory.

Other financial planners might ask in the initial meeting, "When do you want to retire, and how much money do you need to live on?" Those are important questions, and our process tackles them of course—but not right at the beginning. Instead, we begin by getting to know you. This is the second step toward financial health:

STEP 2
EXPLORE FACTS AND FEELINGS

When potential clients first come to meet with my team, our goal is to gather information to understand their unique situation. This means looking at your circumstances from an aerial view and conducting a survey of your life, your goals, and your current situation.

This process involves asking many questions: What's most important to you? What are your goals? Where do you feel you are today in relation to those goals? Where would you like to be? What's not happening that should be happening? What would you like to be different? And, of course, what is the goal you have in mind? *What does financial freedom mean to you?*

Many people learn that financial freedom often includes freedom of time. We don't stop there. Instead, we go to the deeper question: If financial freedom is freedom of time, then what would you do with that newfound time? *What are you passionate about?* This helps us understand you better. Many of my entrepreneur clients say that they would start another business in retirement. To them, financial freedom is the freedom to create and grow another enterprise—perhaps something they've been dreaming about for a long time.

Or would you do volunteer or philanthropic work? Or spend time with family? Some people say, "I'm just going to take a lot of trips with my grandchildren." Others say, "My grandchildren live all over the place, and I'm going to visit them as much as I can." Others want to write a book or finally have time for other creative endeavors. Others act as mentors to other business people or as caretakers and/or influencers for family members or other people in their lives.

This might not sound like it has much to do with financial planning, but it does. These questions and answers aren't a frivolous exercise. The more vivid we can make your goals, the more likely you'll achieve them. The more you can visualize your goals, and the more you say them aloud, from my life experience, the more likely they are to happen. If the dream of having financial freedom means certain things to you that you can hear or see; or you have certain places you want to travel, and you can really picture them; or you have a vision for a project or a charity you want to start or another business that you'd like to pursue, the more clearly you see these things and the more emotion that's attached to them, often comes a better likelihood that they become a reality. These dreams should indeed have emotions attached to them, and they should be connected to the people in your life. All this makes them more vivid and real and more likely to come to fruition. Part of the reason for this has to do with simple motivation: If you have a clear picture in your mind of the future you want, then you're more likely to complete all the necessary steps to get there. This is integral to fiscal therapy.

At its core, this line of questioning has to do with one of the most important things any of us can ask ourselves: What do we really want to do with our lives?

I use these same questions to help clarify goals in my own life. Every year I do a vision board of pictures, and then I keep it on my desk at home. Two years ago, as part of that exercise, I decided that I wanted to have more free time in my life to play music, so I put up a picture of the bass guitar I wanted. This past year, after I'd hit all my goals for my business, I bought that bass. Another goal I had set for myself was to do more charity work. Well, guess what? I'm now part of a band that plays monthly charity events. We don't get paid. We raise money for charity every time we play. All of the sudden I'm fulfilling two goals in one—and I strongly believe that's a direct result of having put those goals on my vision board and looking at them every day.

A friend of mine is a great example of someone who has really visualized exactly what he wants for himself. His name is Ray Loewe, and he started a company called The Luckiest Guy in the World. Ray is not a client of mine. He's passionate about photography and travel, so what he's done is begun organizing and leading trips around the world with people like himself. He recently led a great trip to China with a group of likeminded folks, with the specific purpose of photographing panda bears. He's also started a consulting business to help other people with financial freedom determine what they want the rest of their lives to look like and then to make that happen.

Ray is a bit older than I am, and to me he's a great example of what it means to recreate your life at a later stage. He's now in his seventies, and he has a twenty-five year plan. I think in the same kind of way. I'm looking way beyond the typical life expectancy.

In addition to this kind of visioning, the fiscal therapy

getting-to-know-you process also encompasses the more traditional financial planning questions. A typical planner will ask how much money you need each year in retirement, and my team certainly seeks out that information. But we don't stop there.

Let's say you want $200,000 a year in retirement. Well, you probably don't need all that money at once, and you may need more in certain years and less in others. For instance, maybe you're planning to do a ton of traveling right at the start of your retirement. In that case, your financial needs are front-loaded. Or maybe you're going to settle into retirement for a couple of years and then plan some big trips; in that case, you don't need as much money up front, and we plan accordingly. Most likely this means you need different buckets of money—for the near term, perhaps the midterm, and the long term. You need different buckets for different goals.

We ask about your fears, too. Again, one of the most important things we're doing in fiscal therapy is helping you develop a more peaceful relationship with money. It should no longer be a source of stress and fear in your life. Many people are afraid of the future being worse than today, and money tends to have a lot to do with that. I'm actually a good example of this because I've always had an aversion to living on a fixed income. But I have personally learned that naming the fear and getting it out into the open is an important step toward addressing it because that allows you to come up with an appropriate plan. I've done it for myself. Because I don't want to live on a fixed income, I'm planning various income streams for myself in retirement. I love Ray Loewe's model, in which he's starting new enterprises and consulting in his seventies, and beyond.

Bringing *your* fears out into the open will allow you to come up with plans to address them. That's part of what fiscal therapy is all about. Some people fear that they will no longer be relevant as they age or that their knowledge will no longer be useful. Great ways of addressing those concerns are to keep learning and trying new things at every age. Some people actually use the term *refirement* for reimagining a brighter, more fabulous future. I recently watched Carl Reiner, the great comedian, on *CBS This Morning* talk about a documentary he did called "If You're Not in the Obit, Eat Breakfast." He spoke of his desire not to "retire," but instead "inspire." I LOVE IT! By the way, another legendary comedian, George Burns, who, at eighty-eight wrote the book *How to Live to Be 100*, responded to the question "George, what do you do to live so long?" by saying, "Keep breathing." Many people find that their fears start to fade when they have things they're excited about in the months and years ahead.

For some people, those fears specifically center on health. Many people worry that they're limited by how old their parents were when they passed away. Some clients tell me that their parents died in, let's say, their early sixties, so they feel there's no way that they'll live to have a long and fruitful retirement. But the truth is that no one knows the future. My father is a perfect example. No one in his family lived to be elderly—except him. It might have been because he took better care of himself, or it might have been for other reasons that are hard to put your finger on. He certainly had a great attitude and sense of humor, which I am sure did not hurt! So when people share with me their fears about mortality, I remind them that taking good care of themselves combined with modern medical advances can go a long way toward changing the life expectancy that applied to their parents' generation.

As part of this in-depth process, we also talk about your strengths. In what ways do you feel like you're on track to meet your goals? Are there resources or assets that you have that you'd like to better use to your advantage?

We talk about disappointments, too. If you could change something, what would you change? And how would those changes enhance your life?

We also consider dangers. What are you afraid might get in the way of your achieving your goals? Are you worried about a weak market? Are you concerned that your business might not perform as well as expected? Are you worried about illness or disability?

We then discuss potential opportunities to overcome those dangers, and in so doing, we refer to your strengths.

Then we turn our focus to the future. We ask a version of a question coined by Dan Sullivan, founder of The Strategic Coach Program: "Imagine today's date is _____ (three years in the future). What would have to happen, personally, professionally, and financially, for you to look back at the last three years and feel that this was a successful period of your life?" This is a very open-ended question, and through it, we better understand the "softer" data, the things that the financial numbers can never tell us.

We also use some excellent personality assessment tools to better understand who you are and your approach to money. There are many such tools out there; you might be familiar with Meyers-Briggs, StrengthsFinder, The Disc Profile, or Enneagram. Some of these tools are even used in the hiring practices of Fortune 500 companies. For our fiscal therapy practice, we tend to use

Kolbe, which gauges your natural instincts and talents.

This sort of assessment can be particularly important in helping couples or business partners who are embarking on the fiscal therapy process together. If you have a spouse or a business partner whose natural operating style is very different from your own, that can be a significant obstacle as you try to move forward. For example, in the Kolbe assessment, I'm a high "Quick Start," which means that I deal with uncertainty and risk through innovation and improvisation. On the other side of the coin, you might be a high "Follow Thru," which means that you're great at taking a vision provided by a "Quick Start" and seeing it through to completion. No matter what your particular strengths, and those of your spouse or business partner, we focus on building on those strengths to facilitate a more effective planning process.

It's important to note that this type of personality exploration applies not only to personal finances but also to businesses and business partnerships. If you're a business owner, then this feeling- and fact-finding process encompasses the finances of your business. Just as every individual has a distinct personality, every business has its own "personality," too. Assessing your business culture is an important part of this exploration, and the financial plan that we craft together should include plans both for your own finances and for your business, which should include an exit strategy or succession plan.

An important objective in all this exploration is to uncover your underlying feelings about money. Many of us are afraid of running out of money or we're afraid of what it means to live on a fixed income or we're afraid of a future that's worse than today. These fears are normal. Yet they're also an opportunity—an opportunity that the fiscal therapy process puts to productive use. To once again quote Strategic Coach Dan Sullivan,

Fear + Excitement = Transformation

Fear doesn't have to be a problem or an obstacle; in fiscal therapy, we acknowledge the presence of these very normal fears, and then we use that energy and motivation to endeavor to build a more secure and prosperous tomorrow.

Indeed, too many of us were taught that money is the root of all evil. Consider the case of a good friend of mine who's wildly successful. He's a very accomplished physician with multiple advanced degrees. I went out to dinner with him recently, and I described for him the notion of fiscal therapy as a potential solution for the negative feelings that so many of us have around money. I couldn't believe his response.

"I wish I'd had that," he said. "I'm *still* all screwed up about money."

He went on to describe some of the things his father used to say to him—things that had made him afraid to accumulate wealth, and even more afraid to spend it.

I was astonished. This guy is in his seventies, and he is, by pretty much any standard, extremely successful. And yet he still feels anxious when it comes to money. He still feels afraid.

Interestingly enough, Bruce Springsteen (I'm a big fan!) may present a similar case. In his autobiography, *Born to Run*, he describes the fact that he came from a very poor working-class background. Now, of course, he's a multimillionaire rock star. And that has apparently given him a complicated image of himself. He generally dresses on stage (and in life) as a guy who works in a factory. He seems to do that on purpose because those are the people he feels most connected to. He also, apparently, gives lots of money to charity. He seems to be committed to using his wealth to do good things in the world, of course, but a sense of guilt about the level of his own wealth may also motivate him to give so much away and to publicly in certain ways.

No matter who you are, money can be complicated!

Happily, you're already well on your way to addressing that complication head-on and looking to build the financial wellness that you deserve.

Building Wellness Through Fiscal Therapy

Some people think that the notion of "therapy" sounds intimidating, but it doesn't have to be: Think of massage therapy. This isn't something bad, but rather a matter of getting below the surface to heal physical discomfort and to make you stronger for the future. In fact, one can feel great!

Indeed, the fiscal therapy model of the client-to-professional relationship parallels that of many health professionals. It stresses the importance of getting to know clients at a deeper level, understanding their goals and motivations, assessing their current financial situation, and then developing, recommending, and implementing a strategy designed to meet their objectives. Just as a doctor or physical therapist helps you maintain your health and build strength and resilience, a fiscal therapist helps you maintain your wealth and build strength and resilience for the future. And just as a good physician doesn't recommend a treatment program without doing a thorough assessment, a trusted advisor won't make any planning recommendations without first fully understanding your unique circumstances. In both settings, the advisor carefully assesses your starting place and then creates a tailored wellness plan.

The metaphor extends to the maintenance of your health, or finances, over time. The act of managing your financial life is similar to the way you maintain good physical health through exercise and attention to diet. The doctor or financial advisor helps you implement your wellness plan and then charts progress in the subsequent months and years, checking and correcting along the way. When you're on track and in good health, you only need an annual checkup with your doctor. When you have a financial plan in place, you may only need to check in a couple times a year with your advisor. And when pressing questions arise—whether about your personal circumstances, or about the global economic landscape—you have a trusted professional to call upon, someone who has built a career by studying financial indicators and learning how they will or will not affect individual clients.

Physical therapy, conducted by professionals, does a body good. It brings your muscular and skeletal support systems up to a state of good health that can then be maintained by your own informed exercise. Fiscal therapy is the same. It seeks to keep you and your finances in good health and alignment and strives to help make you continually stronger as you follow the steps of your customized plan. It's an ongoing process of developing fitness around money and financial matters.

"Moneytudes"

We try not to be too deadly serious in the fiscal therapy process. Because one of our goals is to help you develop a new approach to money—in which you worry less and are less stressed—we like to take a step back from the process to have a few laughs about, and give some serious thought to, our attitudes regarding money. I like to use the phrase "moneytudes" to refer to these various attitudes around money. Here are a few you might not have considered:

"Money isn't everything, but it certainly keeps you in touch with your children."

—Alexander Hamilton

"Lack of money is the root of all evil."

—George Bernard Shaw

"Money isn't the root of all evil. Jealousy is."

—Unknown

*"Whoever said money can't buy happiness
simply didn't know where to shop."*

—Bo Derek

*"Money can't buy happiness, but it sure
makes misery easier to live with."*

—Unknown

"A lot of money is tainted. 'Taint yours and it taint mine."

—Attributed to Mark Twain

*"If all economists were laid end to end, they
would not reach a conclusion."*

—George Bernard Shaw

*"Live as though you had a full cup. Not half full
or half empty, but full and running over."*

—Unknown

*"Time is more valuable than money. You can get
more money, but you cannot get more time."*

—Jim Rohn

"Money is better than poverty, if only for financial reasons."

—Woody Allen

*"Money is not the most important thing in the
world. Love is. Fortunately, I love money."*

—Jackie Mason

"Too many people spend money they haven't earned to buy things they don't want, to impress people they don't like."

—Will Smith

"A nickel ain't worth a dime anymore."

—Yogi Berra

"It's good to have money and the things money can buy, but it's good, too, to check up once in a while and make sure that you haven't lost the things that money can't buy."

—George Lorimer

Create a Wellness Team For Yourself— For The Long Haul

Fiscal therapy is helping you live your life in a way that you fully enjoy it. To accomplish that, we assist you in creating a financial team for yourself: you and your spouse (or business partner), an attorney, an accountant, a banker, and your fiscal therapist. Once you put together such a team and begin the fiscal therapy process, you'll likely feel a huge relief, along with a sense of excitement, as you begin to craft a plan to help you realize your dreams.

And that brings us right up to the third step in the fiscal therapy process.

THIS CHAPTER IN BRIEF

▲ The second step in the fiscal therapy process is a detailed exploration of where you stand in your life today along with your goals for the future. This means considering one of the most important questions we can ask ourselves: What do we really want to do with our lives?

▲ If you're a business owner, we apply this detailed fact-finding process to your business. Just as every individual has a distinct personality, every business has its own "personality," too.

▲ Fear doesn't have to be a problem or an obstacle. In fiscal therapy, we acknowledge the presence of fear, and then we use that energy and motivation to build a more secure and prosperous tomorrow.

▲ The fiscal therapy model of the client-to-professional relationship parallels the relationship between a patient and a health-care provider. Fiscal therapy is about developing, recommending, and implementing a financial wellness plan to meet your personal objectives.

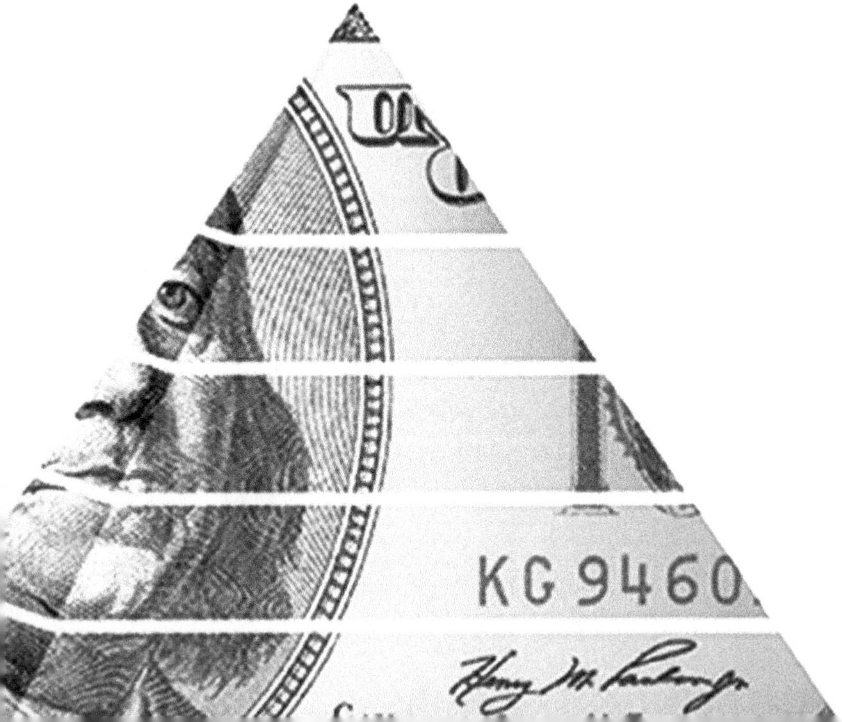
KG 9460

Chapter Three
LET'S HAVE A LOOK

firmly believe that good financial planning does not begin with numbers or calculations. Without a thorough examination of your goals and a qualitative survey of where you stand right now, you will find little meaning in the hard numbers.

But by the third step of the fiscal therapy process, we've conducted that initial exploration. And that's precisely why we're now ready to launch into the quantitative side of things:

CONDUCT A THOROUGH ASSESSMENT OF YOUR FINANCES

At this stage, my team conducts an in-depth review of your facts and figures, including account statements, income statements, business documents, estate planning materials, deeds and titling of assets, and everything else. Here are examples of the typical documents that represent your financial life and that are necessary information for ultimately creating your comprehensive financial plan:

▲ Tax returns

▲ Bank account statements

▲ Savings bonds

▲ Investment products: stocks, bonds, mutual funds, REITs, etc.

▲ Insurance policies

▲ Annuities

▲ Land ownership titles and deeds

▲ Legal documents reflecting inheritance(s) to be gained

▲ Documents that reflect ownership of a business

▲ Statements of liabilities: mortgage, loans, credit balances, college tuition, etc.

▲ Pension plan, 401(k), IRAs, etc.

▲ Wills, powers of attorney, living wills, and health-care powers

▲ Trusts, including any living or irrevocable trusts

Though the idea of gathering (or, in some cases, *finding*) these statements and papers may seem intimidating, the payoff is substantial. Soon you'll be able to view your entire financial life in a single document that summarizes your position and provides recommendations for where to go next. I have observed that the feeling of relief that people gain with that level of organization is, frankly, priceless.

As part of this stage of the process, we contend with the fact that most people tend to accumulate a lot of financial *stuff* over the course of their lives, just the way they accumulate old belongings in their attics. There are old insurance policies that may no longer have a purpose. There are old accounts that may have been long forgotten or that were never really used in the first place. There may be deeds to old family properties. There may be investment vehicles or other financial tools that an enterprising salesperson once convinced you that you needed. Part of the work of the financial planner is to sift through this financial attic, see what's in there, and then provide observations and sound guidance about how to use assets most efficiently according to the client's specific goals and circumstances.

This is also the point in the process in which we begin to do what we call "myth busting." Most people have acquired biases for or against certain financial instruments. Some people might believe, for instance, that life insurance is only for when your kids are growing up, that the lowest-cost life insurance or mutual fund is always the best, or that annuities are always bad because they have high fees. The financial media are constantly spewing this type of advice (and the advice is constantly changing and sometimes even reversing).

Part of the fiscal therapist's job is to bust these myths because the facts about any given financial instrument are invariably more complicated than what the financial media have portrayed. For instance, if you use an annuity to accumulate money without taking an income stream from it—well, then yes, the fees *may* be too high. On the other hand, if you use an annuity, in my view, for the right purpose, which is to create income for yourself at a higher level than you could obtain elsewhere, then it might be like creating your own pension. In some cases, that could be useful. There's also a myth out there that you should always put as much money as you can into your IRA or 401(k). Counteracting that myth is TV personality Ed Slott, a well-known CPA, who says that putting as much money as possible into those tax-advantaged accounts can be a tax trap because you may end up paying all your taxes on the other end, perhaps at higher rates, in retirement. According to Ed's line of thinking, you should consider having as much retirement income free of tax liability as possible.

Which approach is right?

My answer is that it depends. It depends on the person. Financial planning is not a one-size-fits-all science. What you read in the newspaper, or what you hear on TV, may not always be right (and sometimes is dead wrong). Sometimes you'll hear contradictory information, and *both* sides are incorrect. In the case of contributions to retirement accounts, it typically depends on whether your employer is matching your savings. If you have a match, then it usually makes sense to take advantage of that to the extent that you can, as it's essentially free money. If there's no match, then there is a mix of different tools that you can use to defray your future tax liability, as opposed to making tax-free contributions into those retirement accounts today, only to delay your tax bill for a later decade. Everyone's individual situation is unique.

This has to do with yet another myth, which is that your tax rate will be presumably lower in retirement than it is today. In fact, no one knows what future tax rates will be, including Congress. (*Especially* Congress!) Federal and state governments are increasingly relying on what are called "stealth" taxes, which are taxes on items such as health care, or perhaps, retirement plans. An example is the Medicare tax of 3.8 percent on investment income that went into effect on January 1, 2013. In other words, there is evidence that it is possible that you could be taxed at higher, not lower total tax rates in your later years.

As long as we're talking about conventional wisdom, we should also spend a moment on conventional wisdom that's true, as opposed to false. Here's some great conventional wisdom that's attributed to Benjamin Franklin, a larger-than-life legendary icon of US history. Benjamin Franklin said, "Pay yourself first." This is why his face is featured on the cover of this book. The sooner that you start putting your money away and letting it compound, the better off you are. Pay yourself first!

Just a few days ago, I got a phone call from a friend who wanted to know whether he was getting good advice regarding the purchase of a particular financial instrument. "Should I be buying this?" he asked. He wanted me to give him a cut-and-dried answer.

The product in question was a type of annuity. He wanted to know whether he should buy it.

"It depends," I said. "What are you looking to do with it?"

We got into a conversation about products, but the more we talked, the more it became clear that he didn't have a plan for how this product would fit into his larger financial picture.

"I really can't give you a good answer unless we talk about your overall plan," I said at last. This is a great example because accurate answers about financial products generally have less to do with the product itself and might have much more to do with the details of the individual's plan. And in this particular case, when we actually got into the details of his retirement planning, an important finding emerged.

It became clear that his concern was volatility in the markets. "Because of the way his assets were structured, he had left himself exposed to volatility, which can spike sharply in response to political events or changes in the global economic landscape. And this particular person's portfolio was structured around a traditional 60/40 division, with 60 percent in equities and 40 percent in bonds. That division had actually exposed him to much more volatility than he realized. When we got down to it, the annuity was not the top concern. He needed to reorganize for less volatility—and only *then* decide whether to purchase an annuity.

The concern about volatility brings up another important aspect of fiscal therapy: In some cases, it might be appropriate to look beyond stocks and bonds to alternative investments as a form of diversification. Alternatives can include real estate investment trusts, commodities, , "hedge" type funds, energy funds, or a host of other kinds of assets. Many brokers will tell you that you should have no more than 15 percent of your portfolio in alternative investments; they'll say that it's too risky to carry a load any greater than that. This is because these types of funds may be micro-specific and in and of themselves might introduce more risk. But if alternative investments are properly selected and structured, they can in some cases make a portfolio *less* risky. The 15 percent rule for alternative investments is a broad generalization—once again, it's conventional wisdom that glosses over the complexity of the issue. This discussion is not intended as a recommendation, but rather presents a point to consider that the "conventional wisdom" may not always apply to your specific situation.

Financial myths, erroneous financial "wisdom," and red-alert warnings from the financial media all contribute to widespread angst and unease about money. In the fiscal therapy process, we're busting those myths and creating space for ease and wellness.

Your Physical Exam—From the Top of Your Head to the Tips of Your Toes

Just as fiscal therapy in general parallels a good medical checkup or physical therapy regimen, this particular step in the process is like a thorough physical. The fiscal therapist checks out all the "bodily systems" of your current finances.

Income

Streams of income are basic to any financial plan, and there are several: salary, bonuses or profit distribution, investment dividends, rents, and so on. In the medical analogy, your income is your ability to create a flow of money into your life and being. If your income is equivalent to the air you breathe, a financial planner uses a metaphorical stethoscope to examine your monthly disbursement. Are you doing the equivalent of breathing well on your airstream of money? Is your breathing difficult or limited? What could be done to make this process of incoming and outgoing breath/cash better—both for short-term relief and for the long-run health of your lungs/ledgers?

Savings

Ben Franklin said it best: "Pay yourself first". There are enormous benefits to starting as young as possible and putting away 10 to 20 percent of your gross income for future financial independence. Even if you didn't start young, that doesn't mean you can't start now.

The money that's parked in savings is there for a number of reasons: security against market vagaries, loss of income, and unexpected expenses; to expand your business; for use in leisure and celebration; to support a loved one's education; for earning compound interest so your wealth becomes more abundant; to support you during retirement; to leave a legacy for loved ones; and, perhaps, just to know it's there, to provide a sense of comfort. Your ideas and feelings about the act of saving and holding money for the future are discussed at the outset of our relationship.

Debt

Debt management is also an important topic, and I should say that debt is not all bad. For instance, it can provide leverage for important things. The most obvious is the purchase of a home. But it can also be crucial for starting or expanding a business, the acquisition of commercial real estate, and other investments that are in service to long-term financial goals.

At the same time, excessive debt can be dangerous. You're probably well aware that many investors were overleveraged in the run-up to the financial crisis of 2008. Many fortunes were wiped out, and many entrepreneurs had to start over as a result of too much leverage. That's why balance and proper financial guidance in the fiscal therapy process are critical.

Insurance and Risk Management

If you had a money machine that popped out $100,000 a year or more, would you want to insure it in case it ever stopped working? I sure would. This is the essence of disability insurance policies: They provide protection, thereby making your future more secure. As with savings, these policies also may provide peace of mind. They are especially important for those earlier on in their working years, as their greatest financial asset—their ability to earn an income—will continue to grow for many years.

Indeed, insurance is essential for protecting the assets for which you and your family have worked so hard. Your most important assets—your income and your own life—are protected through disability and life insurance. There are myriad types of insurance products, and it's important to find the right types and levels of protection for your circumstances.

To use a tragic example, consider the Wall Street workers and executives who perished on September 11, 2001. I know of several friends of friends who worked at Ground Zero at that time and who did not survive the tragedy. Plenty of stories emerged at that time about highly paid executives whose life insurance was only two times their annual salary. That meant that their families could only live comfortably for a couple of years after losing their dearest loved one. After that, they would need to dramatically change their lifestyles—the last thing they needed after enduring such a loss. Insurance is protection from life's uncertainty, and it's a deeply important matter.

A good financial advisor assists you in evaluating the strength of your protection, helping manage your lifestyle responsibilities, planning for risks, and helping with your later-in-life costs along with how all these things will factor into the legacy you'll leave. Your fiscal therapist lends his or her expertise to these complex matters.

Investments

Investments represent your future strength. They can also be extremely complicated, with varying degrees of risk, potential for growth, and layers of fees. For good reason, many people find that complexity overwhelming. Of course, you don't try to perform your own medical exam; you leave that to your doctor. Here your fiscal therapist applies a lifetime of experience to examining your investments, assessing your strengths and weaknesses, and providing sound guidance.

When you are reviewing your existing finances, and drawing up plans for the future, your approach to risk is an important consideration. For example, if you had a high tolerance for risk when you first began saving and investing, but you've become less risk tolerant over time, it's probably appropriate to make adjustments to your portfolio. Similarly, if your plan warrants a need to be more aggressive and growth oriented, and your risk tolerance allows for it, we may need to shift your balance away from certain types of assets and toward others. It's the job of your fiscal therapist to understand your risk tolerance and your present and future needs and then to help you strike the right balance.

Taxes

Taxes are a fact of life. The earlier you factor them into your financial plan—with strategies to become as tax *efficient* as possible—the better. In developing your plan, we look at the types of taxes you may be paying at present and begin to consider long-term strategies for efficiency.

Estate Planning

Having the guidance of a financial planner in structuring your estate plan is one of the most important reasons to engage in the planning process. My team and I assist clients in establishing goals for their estate and tactics for funding those goals and in planning around tax liabilities and costs of transferring assets to the next generation. This process is performed in coordination with your estate planning attorney and perhaps other members of your team, such as your accountant.

Philanthropy and legacy

How would you like to be remembered? What kind of values would you like your financial resources to represent? If you have accumulated more than enough resources for you and your spouse or partner, then it's time to talk about how you would like your assets dispersed. Would you like to provide for loved ones or apply your resources toward certain causes that may have been important to you in your lifetime?

A financial planner who understands you and your legacy goals can help you create a strategy to share your money for the betterment of your community and do so in a way that reduces your tax liability.

Diagnosis—And a Proposal to Move Forward

After evaluating your overall health and checking all your key indicators, from your pulse and weight to muscle reflexes and blood pressure, your medical professional offers you a diagnosis. So, too, does your fiscal therapist.

After the in-depth review of all your documents and an analysis in the essential areas of income, savings, insurance, investments, risk tolerance, taxes, estate planning, and philanthropy and legacy, my team puts together our observations: our diagnosis of your situation.

Oftentimes what we discover is that there is a disconnect between people's wishes and hopes as compared with what they're actually on track to achieve. It's our job to identify whether such a disconnect exists and then provide guidance on how to correct it. This comes in a proposal to move forward: a recommendation, if appropriate, to establish an ongoing client-advisor relationship.

How It Works In Practice

Here's how the third step of the fiscal therapy process works in practice.

Here is the hypothetical case of Ron and Sylvia. They have two daughters working in the business and a son whom they are talking about bringing into the business as well.

Ron and Sylvia have a general idea of what their business would be worth if they sold it on the open market. They know that it wouldn't be quite enough money for them to live on in retirement; they would be right on the edge. But selling the business on the open market is not their goal anyhow. What they want is to sell it to their adult children. The two know that they can't afford simply to give it to their kids, but they do want to sell it to their kids. Ron is fifty-five years old, and he wants to be out of the business by sixty.

As my team looks into the situation, it becomes apparent that the numbers don't add up. Though the business is growing, it is not so lucrative that it could support their kids' three families, and the sale of it to their kids isn't going to provide enough income for Ron and Sylvia's retirement. They either aren't going to be financially independent after the sale of the business or, if they do sell it to their kids for sufficient money to support their retirement, it appears that it would be very difficult for the kids to pay out that amount and still support three families from the business. That's one of the things that people generally don't include in their calculations: whether a business can viably support the families who are going to be dependent on it.

My team might assist them in doing some accelerated funding to create a sort of retirement fund for Ron and Sylvia—a big step toward the financial independence they want and need. We might also suggest that they find good coaching for their business operations, as their business is in a position to grow and expand. By capitalizing on that, they would be able to grow the business such that they might actually be able to support two and a half families from it (because the parents would have funding for a piece of their retirement already in place), which is more or less what they want to do.

I have had situations that I have dealt with that are similar to Ron and Sylvia's in which my team and I are able to see goals are not lining up with the numbers, and we strive to make recommendations that attempt to set them on the right path. It's our job to help align the goals with some specific recommendations to help people progress toward their objective—where their goals weren't lining up with their numbers—and that's the very essence of fiscal therapy.

Or consider the case of a couple I started working with quite a few years ago: thirty years ago, as a matter of fact, right around the time I began my career as a financial planner.

The following is a hypothetical situation drawn from working with my clients over a thirty-plus-year career. Michael and June are not very good savers. It actually is like a wrestling match just to get the two of them to put away $100 a month. As their advisor, I help them strategize to begin saving in a meaningful way.

"Look, there's some amount you can save that's not going to affect your lifestyle," I would tell them. At the beginning, this amount may only be $100 a month. They, in turn, tell me they can't do any more than that.

After a while, though, they would get into a habit of saving that $100 every month. In the beginning June is not working outside the home. Then she begins to work part time, earning around $8,000 a year.

"Look, you didn't have that salary before," I would tell them. "And you were getting by fine without it. Can you save that salary?"

By now they would grow more comfortable with the idea of saving, so they decide to take my suggestion. They start to save that salary.

My goal in a situation like this is to continually encourage clients like these to make how much they can save on an automatic basis. The "Fiscal Therapy" aspect of this, for me, is getting to know the clients, understanding what motivates them, and suggesting a plan of action in words that make sense to them and that they can implement.

But how would this process work for you? Turn to the next chapter.

THIS CHAPTER IN BRIEF

▲ In the third stage of fiscal therapy, your financial planner conducts a thorough review of your finances.

▲ Part of the work of the financial planner is to sift through, and provide recommendations about, the "financial attic"— the assortment of financial products that most people accumulate over the course of their lives.

▲ "Myth busting" may also be a key part of this step in the process. Most people have acquired biases for or against certain financial instruments, and part of the fiscal therapist's job is to bust these myths because the facts about any given financial instrument are usually more complicated than what the financial media have portrayed.

▲ After an in-depth review of all your documents and an analysis of the essential areas of income, savings, insurance, investments, risk tolerance, taxes, estate planning, philanthropy, and legacy, our team diagnoses your situation.

Chapter Four

WHAT WE NEED TO DO IS . . .

I n this phase of the fiscal therapy process, you'll receive our recommendations for your customized "treatment" plan.

STEP 4
RECOMMENDATIONS FOR HOW TO MOVE FORWARD

It's important that the recommendations you receive are rooted in thorough analysis. That's why our team starts by sharing our observations. These observations might explain that you're saving enough, but not in the right places, or that you're doing a good job saving, but it's not yet quite enough to meet the goals you've specified. For example, if you said you wanted to retire at age sixty with $100,000 a year of income, and we run the numbers, we might find out that your current savings level won't support retirement at age sixty, but working until age sixty-five will get you there. We also include options like saving a specified additional amount of money each year and other options that will get you to your stated goals.

More broadly, there may be a disconnect between what you say you want to achieve and what you're currently on track to achieve at this moment; it's the fiscal therapist's job to identify that disconnect and provide the "therapy plan" for proper alignment.

We then provide an executive summary of your results. In the executive summary, we enumerate various options to help you improve. Of course, behind the observations, and behind the content of the executive summary, are all the calculations and numbers we've run based on the financial documents you have provided; that is, we provide the backing to show how we came up with each observation and recommendation. The executive summary includes our specific recommendations regarding business planning, estate planning, retirement planning, investments, and protection.

Because our clients are busy people with many commitments of their own, we put all this information into what we call a plan of action, which is one or two pages of bullet points organized by date. I like to refer to this as your "RoadMAP" for success. Your "MAP" is your Money Action Plan, and your RoadMAP encompasses goals, mindset, personal accountability, plan of action, and *make it fun*—that is, throughout the fiscal therapy process, we remain focused on what you're excited and passionate about rather than just the facts and figures.

This action plan comes with specific steps and target dates for completion, and that's, in my opinion, one of the greatest advantages of the fiscal therapy process. Without deadlines, items of importance will never be completed. I've seen so many plans that are not implemented because there are no target dates. Goals without deadlines are dreams—but goals with deadlines become achievable.

We also suggest the team that needs to be involved in any given action item. For instance, if the action item is updating estate documents, the team is the client, the attorney, and the fiscal therapist acting as coach. If the action item has to do with retooling investments, it might be our office and the client's investment broker.

By this fourth step in the fiscal therapy process, you're now at the point at which we review and discuss your comprehensive plan in accordance with your particular philosophy and current financial profile and goals. Our conversations will center on why we recommend certain strategies specifically for your financial landscape.

This is a plan that we're building for you, bottom up—starting with protection.

We Turn The Brokerage Model On Its Head

One of the reasons that so many people lack a solid financial plan is that the financial industry for the most part takes a backward approach to planning. Though there are plenty of exceptions, generally speaking, the industry is focused on selling products rather than on helping clients create a plan. Unfortunately, many advisors don't take the time to genuinely determine their clients' goals and aspirations. Instead, they focus on selling products because they view the sale of those products as their core responsibility. The upshot of this approach is that many people end up with a whole mishmash of financial instruments that may or may not fit with what they actually want to achieve.

I call this the "brokerage model," and you'll see it illustrated in the pyramid below. The brokerage model is a method of investing that is best illustrated by a pyramid whose base is liquid money in savings, certificates of deposit, and money market fund investments. Directly above this base is fixed income. Above fixed income are your mutual fund holdings and then stocks; at the top of the pyramid are alternative investments such as real estate, energy bonds, commodities, collectibles, and any other sort of item you own that may have value that could be purchased by others, such as artwork.

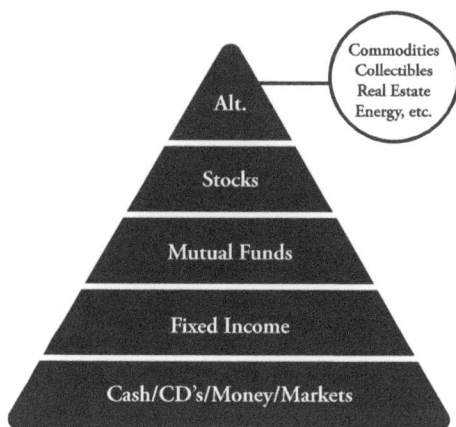

The "brokerage model."

The brokerage model is the bread and butter of companies that earn their profits by selling investments to consumers like you. Financial representatives may first sell clients the safest financial vehicles, which are at the bottom of the pyramid, and then they move up the pyramid toward riskier products that can achieve more growth. But the focus is on the products, and the process is "transactional" in nature.

The fiscal therapy approach, on the other hand, takes a very different tack. We start with goals and dreams and, over the course of the process, turn those goals into actionable plans. The advisor then takes the time to evaluate your strengths and weaknesses and to consider how obstacles can be overcome. Ultimately, the advisor and client together craft a plan to attempt to turn the client's dreams into reality. And over time, as goals and circumstances shift, client and advisor work together to update the plan as needed.

What follows is a second pyramid that shows how fiscal therapy is different from the brokerage model. Notice that the foundation of the pyramid is protection, which is where a good plan starts—something that you can fully appreciate after reading about the story of my dad's business. The last stage of the fiscal therapy process is leaving a legacy. And from the bottom of the pyramid to the top, this process tracks with the life stage of the individual client.

Legacy

Income

Growth

Savings/Debt

Protection

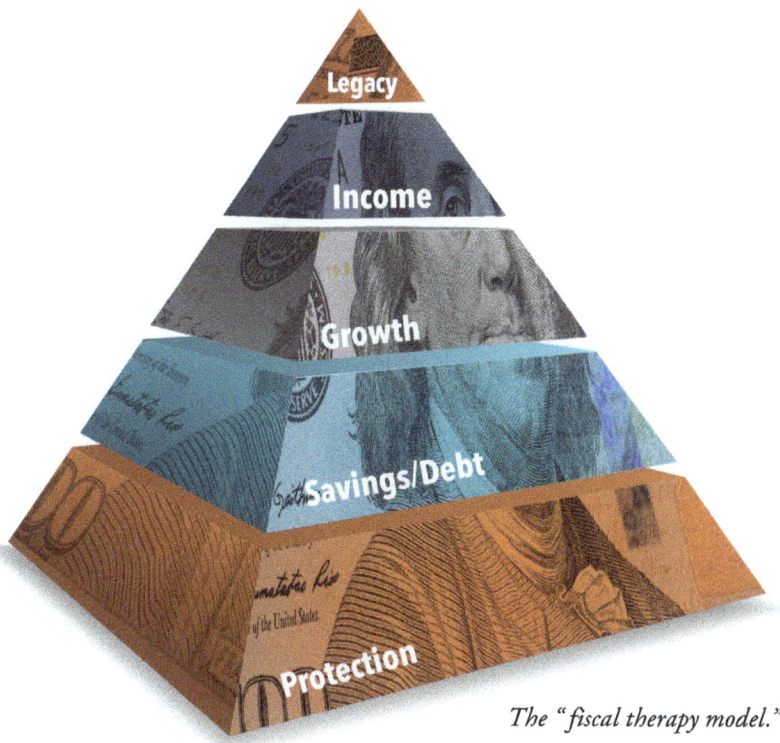

The "fiscal therapy model."

We use this pyramid to model our holistic approach in guiding you through your personal and business financial life. Notice that this approach begins with the concept of "protection" at its base. To give you a feeling of solidity, or solidarity, this is a place where many plans begin. Above that, we look closely at your assets and liabilities. This will serve as the foundation for the best ways to grow your money. Above that, we plan the creation of income sources that will support your financial independence. Finally, we discuss the legacy you want to leave to your heirs.

From bottom to the top, we work together to discuss the types of plans and financial programs that best match your tolerance for risk, your industry or product preferences, the performance of certain investments over time, and what all of that means for your future.

As these illustrations make clear, our approach to accomplishing your goals is very different from the traditional brokerage model.

How It's Worked For People Like You

Consider the hypothetical case of Chuck, a business owner who has a business plan and an investment plan with which he is generally very happy. Chuck's wife is not involved in his business, but she holds ownership in it. At the same time, his son, who has relevant technical training, has joined the management team in the business. Chuck has now become concerned about the existing plan for his company's being inherited in equal measure by his wife, son, and daughter. With the son now employed in the business, Chuck's estate plan may no longer make sense. He wants to change his plan in a way that would take into account the efforts put into the company by his son yet still be fair to his spouse and daughter.

In a situation such as this, we would collaborate with his attorney to help Chuck develop a new plan for his estate that meets all his objectives. We generally create a time line to help him complete his financial plan and legacy plan as he desires.

Then there is the hypothetical situation of Bill and Gina, owners of a plumbing supply company. They have three children: a son and a daughter involved in the business and another son who is not active in the business. The active son, Joe, is the CEO of the company and is running day-to-day activities with some guidance from Bill. Their daughter, Ashley, works for the company in a management role.

As Bill and Gina begin to think about their retirement, they take a harder look at the ownership structure of the business. While they still own the majority interest in the company, they have gifted some stock to all three of their children. Yet it no longer makes sense for Gene, the inactive son, to own an interest in the business; he is a psychologist in private practice and is never going to work in the company.

We might consider working with the company's accountant and estate planning attorney to develop a tax-efficient plan to sell the rest of the business to the two active children while also buying out Gene's interest. Here is where we often hit a snag. Prior to selling, the owners often want to make certain that their financial independence is assured. This requires more planning in areas of cash flow for retirement.

In this case, to go to the next step, we would set about establishing financial goals, including the annual income that would make Bill and Gina comfortable in their retirement. Once we have that number, we can create a buyout plan coupled with a salary continuation plan for Bill that would provide him with financial independence during his and Gina's retirement years. To accomplish all this, we probably would have to work in close collaboration with the existing team of accountants and lawyers.

In another imagined case, Karen and Ted, like Bill and Gina, are also the owners of a family business. They are in their seventies and are largely inactive in the business; their daughter, Christine, has taken the lead. Yet Karen and Ted have not officially retired, and they continue to be involved in business operations on an occasional basis. If they are like many clients, they have ideas on where to go from here. I would start out by trying to understand their ongoing involvement in the business.

I would ask, "Is there any reason you need to continue on in the business?"

"Well, not really," said Karen. "We just want to make sure we're financially independent. We have heard about ESOPs and wonder whether they would be good for us."

I bring up the idea of ESOPs because over the years, many clients have suggested this structure as a possible exit strategy from their closely held business. An ESOP is an employee stock ownership plan. It is a complex tool in which tax advantages may inure to the business owners. It can make sense if the ultimate goal is to have the business owned by the employees of the company as a group. But there is an expression I use that says, "Don't let the tax tail wag the dog." While the tax benefits are great, I suspect that in this case, an ESOP may not be appropriate.

I would recommend a "Fiscal Therapy" style plan for Karen and Ted. Through the planning process, I might discover some of the following.

Karen and Ted want Christine to inherit the business and perhaps have the ability to pass the business on to her children, the next generation. Also, several times when I have asked clients why they are interested in an ESOP, it is because they know someone who sold his or her business to an ESOP and is now living a very nice lifestyle and is happy with the decision.

It could be that Karen and Ted might be able to achieve similar or the same result by gifting or selling the remainder of the business interest to Christine while complementing that transaction with a salary continuation plan, the combination of which could secure their financial plan for retirement.

As we begin to try to straighten all this out, yet another complication could spring up. Sometimes a client has other professional advisors who might be a little defensive because they see our role as infringing on their territory. The rest of this hypothetical situation will outline a situation similar to several I have encountered over the years.

In the case of Karen and Ted, let's suppose they have a lawyer with whom they have worked for many years. He is someone I know from the community. When I call him to discuss our potential solutions, the fact that I know him does not stop him from asking, "What are you going to do for them that I haven't done already?"

Sometimes egos or territorial turf issues like these can crop up. In this situation, I would proceed to talk with him at his office. Let's say that I propose to him that we sell the remainder of the business to a grantor trust (a technique we sometimes use) for the benefit of Christine.

I have had responses such as "That's a recommendation I have made to my clients years ago." It is never my objective to create a problem with another advisor. After agreeing that he is a great counselor and complimenting him on the advice, I quietly ask him, "Well, did they do it?"

A common response would be "No, they didn't." Then I will hear all the reasons for the decision. I would respond with something such as "Please relax; you are their attorney. You're still going to create the documents and agreements on this matter."

The fiscal therapy process helps clients see their entire financial picture. In this case, it would help Karen and Ted to clarify their goals and what it would take for them to exit the business without losing their financial independence. In the process, we would also attach specific planning steps and deadlines to items that otherwise would (continue to) dangle for years. We would help them get an appropriate valuation on their business and help them structure some additional income for their retirement years. Let's take a look at Ellen. She might be someone of considerable means—but as is true with many wealthy people, any change in circumstance can keep her awake at night. Market conditions leave her feeling more vulnerable than she has felt in the past. Then, for personal reasons, she decides that it is time for her to relocate from the town she'd lived in for many years to another part of the country. But her living expenses will increase substantially in her new location, and she becomes concerned that she is extending herself beyond what she can afford. She comes to see us. What she wants out of our meeting is to regain a feeling of security even through changing conditions in the market and in her life.

It turns out that those changes could actually make a considerable difference in her financial standing, and it is good that she has come in for a meeting. We may make some modifications that translate into a greater amount of income for her. We may also segment assets and create different buckets for her based on her needs and timing. This is something we often do for clients. We will help a client like Ellen invest money for short-term needs one way, mid-term needs another way, and long-term needs yet another way. From that structure, we may be able to create a cash flow that specifies when she can withdraw money from which sources. We may also attempt to remove some of the volatility in the way the assets are structured so that conditions may be more stable in the future.

As Ellen begins the process of relocating—which can turn out to be expensive—she can check in with my team once again.

She may want to know whether the financial plan we created is still sufficient. We can go to the numbers again to determine when she might best take money out to accomplish the move. Another hypothetical situation is Howard, a gentleman in his seventies. His concerns are primarily his estate plan, as he has specific bequests that go to certain people. In circumstances like these, I may discover after reviewing estate documents that estate taxes and transfer costs have never been factored into the financial plan. Once those expenses have been factored in, he may have to sell off assets to satisfy the specified bequests.

Howard's situation allows us the opportunity to step back and discuss his vision. We would ask him how he would like to proceed after taking the transfer costs into account. We could reduce the size of the bequests, we could seek more aggressive growth for his resources in the interim, or we could create a new structure to reduce his estate's future tax liability. In these situations, tax planning becomes very important.

Simply creating a trust would not be enough to solve his problem. We may discover that he has already used up his allotment of lifetime gifts in these types of scenarios. He would need to take advantage of legal discounts to get a certain amount of value out of his estate to reduce taxes down the road. One possible strategy in this situation is life insurance. Sometimes we advise clients to gift money into a trust, and then the trust can buy life insurance on their lives; the money then grows inside the insurance policy and can be used to cover estate tax liability. I'd also like to share with you the story of Barb. She isn't my client, but her story sheds light on some of the core values of fiscal therapy. While I was on a business trip, Barb picked me up because she works for a driving service. She asked what I do for work, and I told her. That got us into a long conversation.

"My husband says I'm too focused on money," she told me, glancing back in the rearview mirror.

"Why is that?" I asked.

This was right around the time that I had started writing this book, and I was even more attuned than usual to people's attitudes regarding money.

"I'm so focused on money because I want to make sure we have enough to enjoy it."

She went on to tell me that, right now, all of their vacations involve going camping. One of her goals is to have vacations in which she doesn't have to cook and sleep on the ground during her time off. It sounded like a pretty reasonable plan to me.

Her motivation to get her finances in order came in part from her family. Her father had owned a business, but he had died without a succession plan in place. Her mother had tried to run the business for a while, but she didn't have the right skills or experience to do it, and the family had to close it down within a year.

At that time, Barb and her fiancé were working in the business. So all of the sudden the two of them were out of a job. Her fiancé also had over $10,000 of debt, which she ended up taking over and paying off. Later, their relationship dissolved. Between losing her job and paying off her ex's debt, Barb found herself in pretty bad financial shape. She had also learned a lot from the example of her father's owning a business but passing away without a plan for what would happen to it.

After going through all of that, Barb had become very clear that she never wants to go through anything like that again. She's now married to someone else, and she's taken the lead with her new husband to make sure they're not carrying debt. She makes sure they pay themselves first; they're saving off the top. And to support her financial goals, Barb had decided to take on a second job as a driver, which was how I'd met her in the first place. That wasn't her primary job. She had a full-time job as well.

All of that had happened to her because other people in her life hadn't had proper plans in place. And that's why fiscal therapy is so powerfully important.

THIS CHAPTER IN BRIEF

▲ In the fourth stage of fiscal therapy you'll receive a "diagnosis" in the form of an executive summary with recommendations. This document covers retirement planning, business planning, estate planning, protection, and all other areas of your financial life.

▲ You'll receive a "RoadMAP" for success, in which your "MAP" is your Money Action Plan. Your RoadMAP encompasses goals, mindset, personal accountability, plan of action, and *make it fun*—that is, throughout the fiscal therapy process, we remain focused on what you're excited and passionate about, rather than just facts and figures.

▲ Your action plan will include specific steps and target-dated-for-completion deadlines because goals without deadlines are dreams—but goals with deadlines are achievable.

Chapter Five

THIS WON'T HURT A BIT

The next phase of fiscal therapy is implementation. This is where the "treatment" happens.

STEP 5

IMPLEMENT THE PLAN AND THE TECHNOLOGY CONNECTION

After you've met with a doctor and have had a comprehensive exam, after the doctor has drawn up a personalized treatment plan, and after the two of you have discussed it accordingly, it's time to put that plan into action. When you go in for physical therapy—to strengthen an injured leg, say—that's when the rubber hits the road. The therapist takes you step-by-step through the exercises and stretches that will help you heal previous weaknesses and build strength for the future.

That's precisely what a fiscal therapist does. It's our job to take you step-by-step through the implementation of your plan to meet the goals that you stated at the outset of the process. If we don't assist you throughout this process, then we haven't done our job. If there are parts of your plan that you're not ready to undertake, as is often the case, then we divide your action plan into a current plan and a future action plan. We attempt to not allow goals to drop off the radar simply because today is not the right moment to work on them.

In most cases, the creation and implementation of a financial plan may take up to a year. In the first two to four months, we're getting to know you. In the next six to eight months, we create and begin to implement your plan. During implementation, some of the changes you'll go through will be challenging, whereas others will be easy. But your attitude toward money at any given point in time is what your advisor cares about most.

By the end of the first year, all parts of the plan are in place or are flagged for implementation at a specific time in the future.

This fifth step in the fiscal therapy process also involves setting up certain digital tools to help you over time. We use a digital system that aggregates everything the client owns. It gathers all of their investment accounts, regardless of whether they're at different brokerage houses. It also aggregates their real estate, bank accounts, and business interests, putting everything in one place so the client can see all of it at once. Through this portal, we also set up alarms and alerts for things that need to be done. For instance, if the client's asset allocation goes out of balance because one group of investments is growing faster than another is, we and the client get a reminder to rebalance.

This tool also allows us to automate parts of the action plan so that you receive scheduled reminders to make sure you're on track to meet your goals. You might receive an e-mail that says, "Hey, in three weeks you wanted to have your estate plan done. How are you doing with that?" For someone else, it might be a reminder to finalize a disability insurance policy and for someone else, a reminder about reallocating investment assets. As with all parts of fiscal therapy, it's customized to the details of your particular plan.

At this stage, we also start to measure your progress against benchmarks and goals. I strongly believe that measurement is an essential part of planning because progress that's reported and measured tends to improve exponentially. We check progress quarterly and at least annually to see where you stand in relation to your goals, and this can improve the odds that you'll get the results you want.

This is also an important area in which I believe the old "brokerage model" falls short. Brokers tend to get together with clients on an annual basis to say, "Here's how your investments performed over the last year. Here's what the index did, and here's what you did." They might say, "You're better than the index." Or "You're slightly under the index, and here's why." Sometimes that's all that is examined.

What may matter more is how your portfolio performs on a long-term basis relative to your goals. Are you on track, or are you not on track? That's what matters. In fiscal therapy, we look at your results visually and benchmark your performance against your history and objectives. We say, "Your performance was good relative to your goals or performance was not, and thus you need to save more money to help you get back on track or you are not on track to meet your goals, and therefore we need to reevaluate and adjust accordingly."

With a Plan In Place, You Can Focus On What Matters Most

Suppose Robbie and his wife, Arlene, accumulate a lot of assets over the years and eventually become very well off. In this story, fifteen years ago, they were more focused on estate planning, which can be a very complex and time-consuming process.

Over time, with that plan in place, they are now able to turn their focus to their longest-term bucket: their legacy. They have time and freedom to consider what they plan to leave their grandchildren and future generations. They start thinking more about philanthropy.

Robbie is the one driving this new focus and has a particular interest in supporting a college with which he's affiliated. Thanks to the fact that his financial affairs are in good order, we have a good idea about how much money is available for him to commit to charitable purposes. He is excited that he will be able to make a large commitment to this college. He knows that his money will be used for a cause that he cares a great deal about.

Implementation of a financial plan is really a process that assists in pursuing and achieving dreams and goals. For some people, this means eventually selling their business and using their time to travel; for others, it means having the financial freedom to spend more time with loved ones. For still others, it means *starting* a new business that they've always dreamed about. Everyone is different, which is why we build customized plans—and then help each individual or each family realize its unique goals.

From this point on, the fiscal therapy process is a matter of reviewing and modifying your financial plan as necessary and at year anniversaries.

Over time, of course, your attitude toward money may evolve, and your own goals and priorities may shift. We amend your plan as necessary. Through such changes, your financial advisor is able to provide "institutional memory." The more your advisor knows about you and your history, the better he or she can help you achieve your goals.

THIS CHAPTER IN BRIEF

▲ In the fifth stage of fiscal therapy, we take you step-by-step through the implementation of your financial plan.

▲ We use digital tools to facilitate the implementation of your plan over time, in particular by aggregating all of your assets so that they're visible on one digital page, and to set up reminders to ensure that you're on track to meet your goals.

▲ At this stage, we start measuring your progress against stated goals. Measurement is an important part of planning because progress that's measured and reported tends to be more likely to show improvement.

▲ Over time, your attitude toward money will evolve, and your own goals and priorities will shift. That is a natural part of the process, and we amend your financial plan accordingly.

Chapter Six

SEE YOU IN THREE TO SIX MONTHS

At this point in the process, the hard work is behind you. All that remains is the final phase of fiscal therapy:

STEP 6

CHECK BACK, REVIEW, AND CONTINUALLY READJUST

Once you've worked with a physical therapist on becoming strong and healthy, the time will come when the therapist will give you a clean bill of health. Now he or she only wants to see you every few months, or annually, to review how you're doing—and to determine whether anything has changed or needs to be tuned up.

Well, a fiscal therapist does the same thing. At this point you've followed the treatment plan, and the results are visible: Your health has improved. Now it's a matter of maintaining the good health that you've developed and checking back to adjust as needed.

You now have a dashboard on which you can see every part of your financial life consolidated in a single place. You have the benefit of the technology connection, which turns the planning process from something one-dimensional into a living, breathing organism. It's active; it's not just a sheet of paper. It's changing daily. And as time progresses, there are reminders about things you need to do to maintain your financial health and continue to move in the direction of your goals.

Take a moment to think back on where you were before you began fiscal therapy. You felt uncertain about your finances. Money was a source of worry and anxiety. Now, however, you may feel a sense of comfort and ease. You have a clearly defined plan for financial independence. You know where you stand. You are confident that if you keep saving the amount of money that you're saving, if you keep investing the way you're investing, and if you keep doing all the things you're doing, you may be able to live comfortably for the duration.

In our follow-up meetings, we review all of your details to confirm that you're still on track. We make any corrections or improvements to keep you heading where you want to go. Additionally, when the time is right, we refer to the "future action plan" that we drew up earlier in the process. Recall that there might have been parts of your plan that you weren't ready to implement when we began this process. Well, we keep those plans in our system. When you come in for your checkup, that future action plan is one of the first things we address.

Those plans at one point represented far-off goals or dreams, but thanks to the fiscal therapy process, they soon become current action items—and then, if all goes according to plan, they become reality.

The Sense of Well-Being That You Deserve

I went through several drafts of this book, and that process helped me distill my core purpose and message. I didn't write this book to sell something, but rather to advocate for a process that will help you achieve your goals, whether they are goals for your lifetime or for your legacy and whether they have to do with hard numbers or personal dreams. Throughout this book I've made an analogy between financial planning and health care, and just as you wouldn't consider foregoing health care, the important thing when it comes to your financial goals is that you wouldn't consider going it alone without the counsel of a trusted advisor.

"Fiscal therapy" is a cute name, but it refers to something quite serious. No matter who you are or what goals you may have, what's crucial is that you follow a sound process and that you do so with an advisor you trust—someone who can lend expertise to your unique situation. If you happen to be a financial advisor reading this book, then I want to help you make sure that you have an effective process in place by which you work to understand your clients and their goals and through which you provide them solutions rather than simply conduct asset management and/or sell products.

As it happens, I just revised my own estate plan a few months ago. I had realized that there were things in it that needed to be cleaned up and updated, and thinking about it had started to weigh on me. I worked with my own team on the plan and then with my attorney. When it was done, I felt peace of mind: I now know that everything is just as it needs to be. I know that my family will be okay no matter what happens. I feel a huge sense of relief and well-being because of that.

Today, another hypothetical client, John, came into my office. He has been with me for many years. We began to work on some of his estate planning. Then, lo and behold, he just had twin grandbabies arrive in the world. Their births have changed his perspective on everything. Even though the grandchildren are still babies, the most important thing to him now is to consider the legacy he'll leave for them. That becomes our top priority—to help him find peace of mind in knowing that he's taking care of the next generation in the way that he would like. My goal as a fiscal therapist is to assist you in this same way. It's my mission to help you cultivate that same sense of well-being and peace of mind. *That's* what motivated me to write this book. I set out to offer a new way of thinking about money and its place in your life.

My philosophy is, ultimately, quite straightforward. As an advocate for financial responsibility, I employ the fiscal therapy process to encourage clients to consider financial issues in new ways and from new perspectives. As a result, the client and the planner are both motivated and empowered to explore issues in greater depth, with the objective of crystallizing financial goals and then developing and executing a plan to achieve them.

I have established a vision and principles that we use in my practice, which, I believe, are consistent with the philosophy outlined above.

VISION

We Listen:

We practice fiscal therapy by helping our clients identify and clarify specific objectives and achieve their financial goals. Utilizing a well-defined, consistent planning PROCESS enables us to take advantage of our arsenal of intellectual capital.

We Care:

We use state-of-the-art technology and a dedicated team of hands-on client-service specialists to help our clients implement and maintain their customized financial strategies.

We Serve:

We strive to deliver unexpected and exceptional top-tier client service on an ongoing basis. We serve our clients above all others.

PRINCIPLES

We listen and care

so we can be responsive to the needs of our clients.

We are independent,

having no obligation to anyone except the clients we serve.

We exercise the highest ethical standards,

making recommendations to our clients that we would give to ourselves under the same circumstances.

We plan first

and make recommendations second.

We have built systems and trained our staff

to deliver unexpected levels of service throughout our organization.

With this approach, I built a boutique financial services firm. I built it on the values of listening to clients and helping them identify and clarify specific financial and life objectives. My team helps them design their unique financial plans based on the stages of their financial lives and then implement those plans over time.

I believe in a team approach to financial planning: genuine collaboration between individuals and their trusted advisors. It's only through such collaboration that the process of fiscal therapy is possible.

Wishing you continued fiscal health and success.

If you'd like more information, visit:

TheFiscalTherapySolution.com

Or, e-mail us directly:

marc@thefiscaltherapysolution.com
heather@thefiscaltherapysolution.com